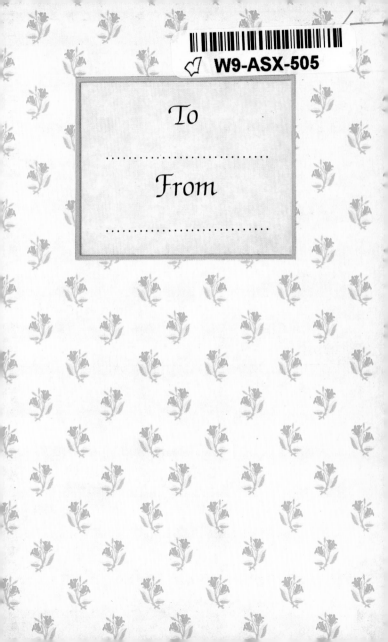

To

....

From

....

A BOUQUET *FOR* MOTHER

Compilation copyright © Orbis Publishing Limited, 1986

First published in 1986 by
Orbis Publishing Limited, London

This book was created by
Eldorado Books Limited, London,
and was designed by Linda Cole.
The illustrations are the work of
Russell Barnett, Grahame Corbett and Sally Kindberg.

Library of Congress Cataloging in Publication Data
Main entry under title:
A Bouquet for Mother
1. Mothers – Literary Collections. 2. English Literature.
3. American Literature. I. Farr, Virginia.
PR1111.M57B68 1986 820'.8'03520431 85-45767
ISBN 0–06–015591–4

Printed in Spain by Printer I.G.S.A. Barcelona

A BOUQUET FOR MOTHER

EDITED BY VIRGINIA FARR

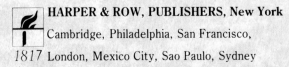

HARPER & ROW, PUBLISHERS, **New York**

Cambridge, Philadelphia, San Francisco,

1817 London, Mexico City, Sao Paulo, Sydney

respect

loving
thoughts

This is the time dear Mother
for me to let you know,
You're thought about more lovingly
than any words can show;
A time as good as any
for me to say anew,
I pray for all the joys of life
to be bestowed on you.

Mother is a word that says
    so very, very much,
It brings to mind a sunny smile,
    a loving, tender touch.
Caring, putting others first,
    concern and patience too,
So many things that make the word
    so special – just like you.

A mother's heart is patient
and understanding too.
A mother's heart can always tell
the considerate thing to do.
A mother's heart is loving
every day throughout the year,
And that's what makes a mother
someone who's especially dear.

'He who goes a-mothering finds violets in the lane.' Just as naturally as the wild flowers sprang from the rough, untended hedgerows of the Middle Ages, so the custom of celebrating Mothering Sunday grew from the harsh realities of life in that period. The fourth Sunday in Lent became known as Mothering Sunday, probably on account of the Epistle for that day which refers to 'Jerusalem . . . the Mother of us all.'

Sons and daughters in service would be given the day off to visit their mothers, taking with them gifts of flowers, simnel or wheaten cakes, or perhaps sugar plums. Daughters would cook the dinner while mother went to church. The custom is ancient, and home-grown from English soil.

In modern times Mothering Sunday has become confused with Mother's

Day, an essentially American custom
that is celebrated in the United States on
the second Sunday in May. This was
instituted in 1907 and ratified by
Congress in 1914.   *Kathleen Jarvis*

Mother is the word for things like this –
   A helping hand, an affectionate kiss,
A loving look and a listening ear,
   Love that grows with every year,
An encouraging smile, a bit of advice.
   Yes, Mother is the word for everything
                    nice!

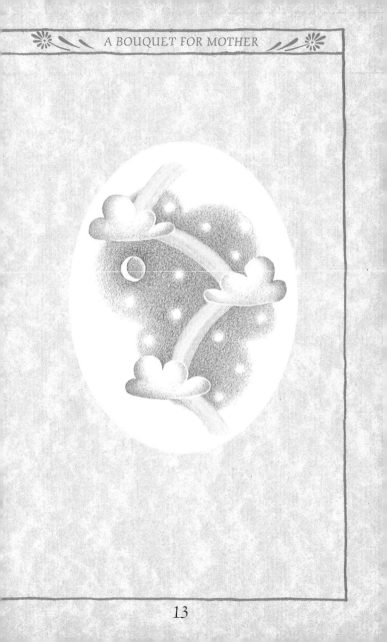

This simple verse says thank you
    for your patience and advice,
The thoughtful things you always do,
    your help and sacrifice.
It brings so many memories
    too special to forget,
Of the love you've always given,
    the example you have set.

A good mother gives her children a feeling of trust and stability. She is their earth. She is the one they can count on for the things that matter most of all. She is their food and their bed and the extra blanket when it grows cold in the night; she is their warmth and their health and their shelter; she is the one they want to be near when they cry. She is the only person in the whole world or in a whole lifetime who can be these things to her children. There is no substitute for her.

Katharine Butler Hathaway

How warmly you love
    and how freely you share.
How gladly you help
    and how deeply you care.

How often you smile
    and how seldom you frown.
There must be just hundreds
    of stars in your crown!

There's a circle of love
that surrounds us,

A bond made of
memories and sharing,

And the wonderful
feeling it fosters

Is warm with
a mother's caring.

Trust always
in a mother's love,
for whatever life may bring,
her special gifts will always be
a very precious thing.

Millions of stars
   in the heavens above,

Only one mother
   to cherish and love.

Thousands and thousands
   of flowers and trees,

Hundreds and hundreds
   of mountains and seas.

Everything's multiplied
   over and over.

Robins and butterflies,
   bees in the clover,
   Many good friends
   to think the world of,
   But only one mother
   to cherish and love.

Our Father in Heaven
    whose love is divine,
Thanks for the love
    of a Mother like mine,
And in Thy great mercy
    look down from above
And grant this dear Mother
    the gift of Your love.
And all through the year,
    whatever betide her,
Assure her each day
    that You are beside her.
And, Father in Heaven,
    show me the way
To lighten her tasks
    and brighten her day,
And bless her dear heart
    with the insight to see
That her love means more
    than the world to me.

Helen Steiner Rice

The selfless and most thoughtful ways,
    The warmth that brightens passing days,
The heart most loving and most true –
    All of these belong to you.

A mother is a combination
   of many wonderful things,
A smile that warms like sunshine
   and gives our troubles wings,
A heart that's full of gentleness
   and love beyond compare,
Hands that soothe and comfort
   when hurt is hard to bear . . .

Eyes that see the good in us
　　and overlook the bad,
Lips that speak warm words of praise
　　to make a heart feel glad.
A mother is a combination
　　of gifts we all possess
And uses them to brighten life
　　and spread true happiness.

As Mothering Sunday is an ancient custom, so simnel cakes have a long history too. Early simnel cakes bore the figure of Christ and Mary and were strictly intended to be eaten on Mothering Sunday. In more recent times they have become identified with Easter and are often adorned with Easter chicks.

The earliest simnel cakes were made with a crust of fine flour deeply coloured with saffron and filled with the usual ingredients for a rich plum cake. This was tied in a cloth and boiled for many hours, unwrapped, coated with egg and baked hard. In later years the crust was replaced by almond paste. The name is thought to be derived from the Latin 'simanellus', the fine flour used in the crust.

Kathleen Jarvis

A mother means something different
    to everyone, I guess.
To me a mother is someone
    who will share my happiness
And listen to my problems
    in an understanding way,
Someone I can count on
    to help brighten up my day.
Someone nice to think about
    whether near or far.
To me a mother is someone
    who is all the things you are.

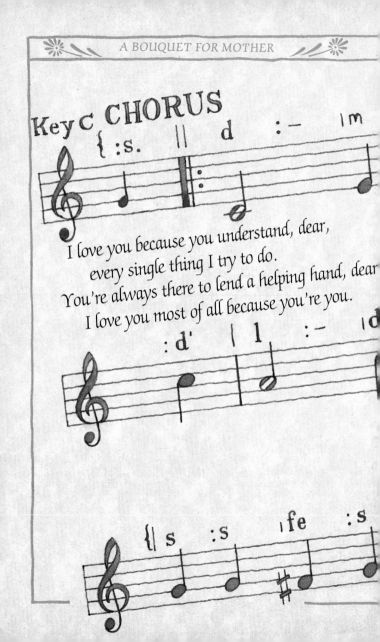

Key C CHORUS

{ :s. ‖ d :— |m

I love you because you understand, dear,
every single thing I try to do.
You're always there to lend a helping hand, dear
I love you most of all because you're you.

: d' | l :— | d

{ ‖ s :s | fe :s

No matter what the world may say about me,
I know your love will always see me through.
I love you for the way you never doubt me,
but most of all I love you 'cause you're you.

Leon Payne

Dear Mother

Throughout your life
may every happiness come your way,
For you deserve life's rich rewards
on every single day.

For permission to reproduce copyright material the publishers
thank Andrew Valentine Ltd; Hallmark Cards; Hutchinson and
Co for the verse from *Loving Thoughts From Helen Steiner
Rice*; and Bourne Music for the verse from 'I Love You
Because' by Leon Payne. Thanks are also due to Candida Twiss.